I draw, I paint

tempera

W9-DFI-676

Text: Isidro Sánchez

Translation: Suzanne Zavrian
Paintings: Vicenç Ballestar
Illustrations: Jordi Sábat
Editorial Direction: José M. Parramón Homs

English translation © Copyright 1992 by Barron's Educational Series, Inc.,

© Parramón Ediciones, C.A. 1992
Published by Parramón Ediciones, S.A. Barcelona, Spain

The title of the Spanish edition is *Mis primeros pasos en témpera*

All rights reserved.
No part of this book may be reproduced in any form, by photostat,
microfilm, xerography, or any other means, or incorporated into any
information retrieval system, electronic or mechanical, without the written
permission of the copyright owner.

All inquiries should be addressed to:
Barron's Educational Series, Inc.
250 Wireless Boulevard
Hauppauge, New York 11788

Library of Congress Catalog Card No. 92-22073

International Standard Book No. 0-8120-1373-5

Library of Congress Cataloging-in-Publication Data

Sánchez Sánchez, Isidro.
   [Mis primeros pasos en témpera. English]
   Tempera : text, Isidro Sánchez ; artist, Vincenç Ballestar ; illustrations,
Jordi Sábat ; translator, Suzanne Zavrian.
      p. cm. — (I draw, I paint)
   Translation of : Mis primeros pasos en rotuladores.
   ISBN 0-8120-1373-5
   1. Tempera painting.   I. Ballestar, Vincenç. II. Sábat, Jordi. III. Title.
IV. Series: Sánchez Sánchez, Isidro. I draw, I paint.
ND2465.S26   1992
751.4'3–dc20   92-22073
                                  CIP

Printed in Spain
2345   987654321

I draw, I paint

tempera

The materials, techniques, and
exercises to teach yourself
to paint with tempera

BARRON'S

What is...

Tempera or gouache?

Tempera and *gouache* are different terms used for the same painting material. *Poster paint* is another variation. All three are *opaque*, water-based paints. You have probably already painted with tempera because it is a technique often used at school.

This volume in the *I Draw, I Paint* series will introduce you to the materials needed for using tempera. It will then teach you the basic techniques for working with tempera. Finally, it will guide you to the creation of finished works of art.

Once you have mastered the technique, tempera paints—in cakes, jars or in tubes—brushes, and a few additional materials are all that you need to paint pictures like the landscape on this page.

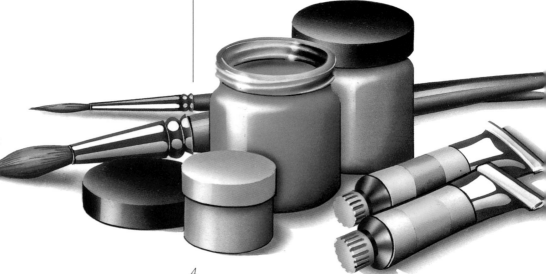

4

Tempera paints are opaque

Just like watercolor paints (see the book on watercolors in this series), tempera paints are diluted with water.

But there are differences between the two techniques.

Watercolors are thin and *transparent*. Tempera paint is thick and opaque. With these differences in mind, you can understand the basic characteristics of tempera painting:

- Tempera paints are opaque. Therefore any color, even a light one, that is superimposed over a darker one, will cover it.
- It is not necessary in tempera painting, as it is in watercolor, to apply light colors first and then the darker ones. The usual order in tempera is dark tones, medium tones, light tones.
- In watercolor painting, white is the white of the paper. When working with tempera, opaque white paint is used.

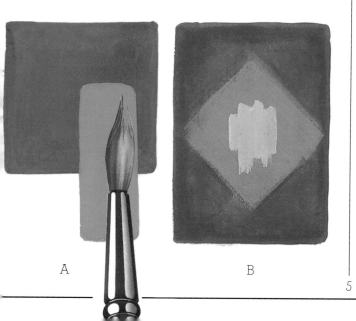

A   B   C

THE BASIC CHARACTERISTICS OF TEMPERA
A. The colors are opaque; therefore, you can paint light colors over dark ones.
B. You can apply a dark tone first, superimpose a medium tone, and finish with a light color.
C. White can be painted over any color.

What I paint with...

Tempera paints

Tempera paints come in cakes, tubes, and jars.

- **Cakes.** Cakes come in boxes of 6 to 16 assorted colors. The cakes can be either square or round and come in different sizes.

   Cakes of tempera are very similar to cakes of watercolor. If you dilute the paint with a lot of water, you will get thin, transparent wash very much like a watercolor. If you apply tempera very thickly, with very little water, you will have a paint that is more opaque. The most opaque tempera is from tubes or jars.
- **Tubes.** Small, medium, and large tubes are available. They can be purchased individually or in boxed sets. These paints are very opaque.
- **Jars.** Jars come in small and large sizes. The large size is recommended for the most often-used colors, such as white. (Jars are less expensive than tubes.)

As you can see, above, tempera comes in tubes of different sizes. Your tubes of white should be the largest size.

LIGHT YELLOW

LIGHT GREEN

The jars of tempera below include the basic colors you will need.

DARK GREEN

OCH

How to use the paints

- **Cakes**. If you paint with cakes of tempera, you can mix the colors in the lid of the box. This is an advantage, but it means that you must clean the inside of the lid before you mix other colors. Also, when you stop painting, you must clean the lid before you put the box away.

- **Tubes.** The best way to get paint out of a tube is by pressing down from the end, rolling it up as you use it.

  When you have as much paint as you need, you must cover the tube as soon as possible.

  Don't take paint directly from a tube with a wet brush. The paint must be squeezed into a dish or some other suitable container.

- **Jars.** Don't take paint directly from a jar. Use the brush or a flat stick to transfer some paint to a dish. If necessary, mix paints in the dish to get the color you need. Then take paint directly from the dish with a clean brush.

LIGHT BLUE DARK BLUE WHITE RED BLACK

When working with cakes of tempera, you can mix the paints in the lid of the box.

7

What I paint with...

Different kinds of brushes

Brushes can have soft or stiff hair. Among the soft-hair brushes, sable is the best. However, less expensive hair and synthetic brushes are available.

What brushes should you have?

Brushes come in different thicknesses, which are easy to identify by the number stamped on the handle.

In the beginning, purchase three round brushes—sizes 4, 6, and 12.

How to take care of your brushes.

- Never let paint dry on the brush. When you finish using a brush, clean it with soap and water and let it dry in a container *with the hair pointing up.*
- Don't leave brushes sitting in a jar of water.

There are round brushes and flat brushes. Only round brushes can be shaped into a point.

FLAT BRUSH   ROUND BRUSH

Use round brushes, numbers 12, 6, and 4.

NUMBER 12

NUMBER 6

NUMBER 4

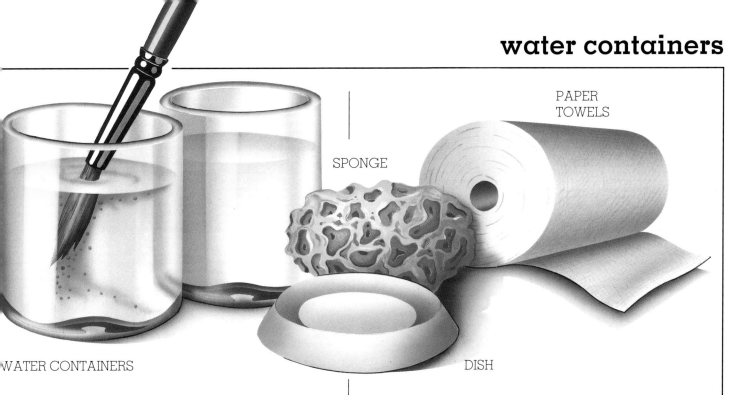

SPONGE

PAPER TOWELS

WATER CONTAINERS

DISH

Brushes and other material

Water containers can be either plastic or glass, but they must have a wide mouth.

It is best to work with at least two containers.

One container is for dirty water—wash the brush in this one before changing colors. The other one is for clean water—dip the brush in this one before taking up paint.

If you use only one container, the water will soon become dirty. This will muddy your colors.

Additional materials

If you use tempera from tubes or jars, you must have one or two dishes in which you can mix colors.

A sponge is very useful for cleaning brushes and even for moistening them slightly when you want to use very thick paint.

Paper towels are used for wringing excess water out of brushes and for drying them after they've been washed.

What I paint with...

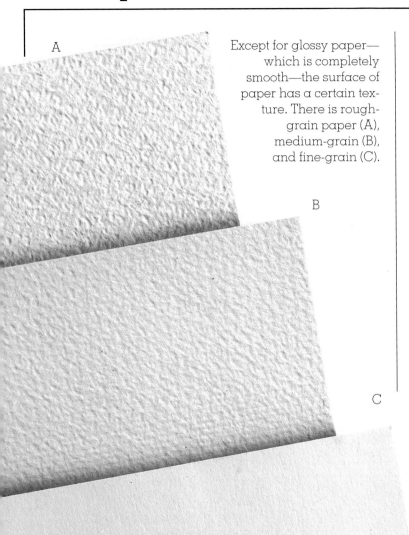

A

Except for glossy paper—which is completely smooth—the surface of paper has a certain texture. There is rough-grain paper (A), medium-grain (B), and fine-grain (C).

B

C

What do I paint on?

The opacity of tempera allows you to work on a variety of surfaces. The most common ones are:

Paper

This is the most frequently used material for drawing and painting with tempera.

The paper you use must meet the following requirements:

- It must be thick enough to avoid warping and puckering when the paint is very wet.
- The paper may be fine-grain, medium-grain, coarse, or glossy. Very glossy paper, however, which has no grain, repels water-based paints.

What I paint on

Paper comes in different forms:

- **Sheets.** There are different size sheets, but the most common is 18 × 24 inches (in metric sizes, 50 × 70 cm). Several different thicknesses are also available.
- **Illustration board.** Since the paper surface is laminated to a rigid support, moisture won't warp it.

- **Pads.** There are several sizes and styles. All are mounted on a cardboard backing; some have a spiral binding. Choose a pad with fairly thick sheets if you apply your paint heavily. A watercolor pad is best if you thin your paint with a lot of water.

Paper may be bought in single sheets or in a pad. Various sizes and thickness are available.

How I paint...

How to apply color

Your first exercise will be to practice picking up paint and applying it to the material you are painting on.

If you are using cakes of tempera, first wet the brush in one of the water containers and then take up the paint from the cake.

If you are using tubes of tempera, squeeze some paint into a dish or onto a palette, wet the brush, and then pick up the paint.

When you are using jars, try to transfer a fairly large amount of paint to the dish, but not so much that it drips.

Before applying color, press the brush against the edge of the dish to get rid of the excess paint.

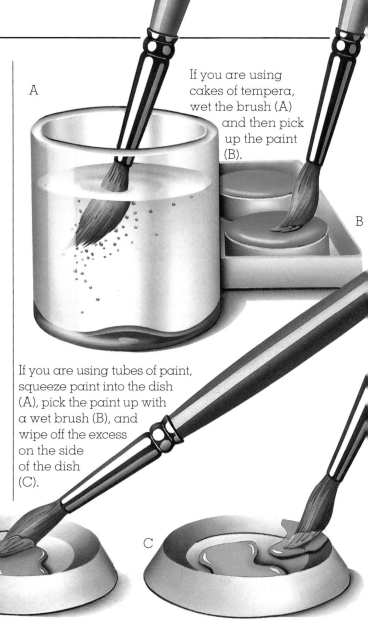

A

If you are using cakes of tempera, wet the brush (A) and then pick up the paint (B).

B

If you are using tubes of paint, squeeze paint into the dish (A), pick the paint up with a wet brush (B), and wipe off the excess on the side of the dish (C).

A

B

C

With tempera you can get lighter or darker tones of a color by adding more or less water.

Tempera or watercolor?

If you use tempera in cakes, and dilute it with enough water, you can paint with a technique similar to watercolor.

If you thin out the paint with water, you will get a light *tone*. If you use less water, the tone will be stronger.

True tempera

However, true tempera is applied with thick paint. In this technique, water is used only to make the paint thinner or thicker.

Then how do you lighten or darken tones? By adding more or less white. And, also, by mixing the color with a lighter color to make it lighter, or a darker color, if to darken it.

Another way of lightening or darkening colors is by adding a larger or smaller quantity of white.

TONE WITH A
LOT OF WATER

WITH A SMALL
AMOUNT OF WHITE

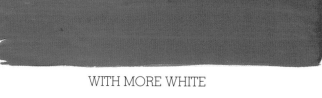

WITH MORE WHITE

WITH A LOT OF WHITE

TONE WITH A DRIER BRUSH

How I paint...

Painting a uniform tone

Begin by extending the color with all the brushstrokes going in the same direction.

Without waiting until this base is dry, superimpose another layer of color, with the brushstrokes going in the opposite direction.

Before practicing this, note these important points:

- Try the wet paint on a piece of paper to check the tone.
- Paint quickly. Tempera dries very fast. You must do this exercise rapidly in order to work while the paint is wet.

Paint a background of a uniform color, with all the strokes in the same direction. Then paint a second coat of color, with all the strokes going in the opposite direction. Work quickly, before the first coat dries.

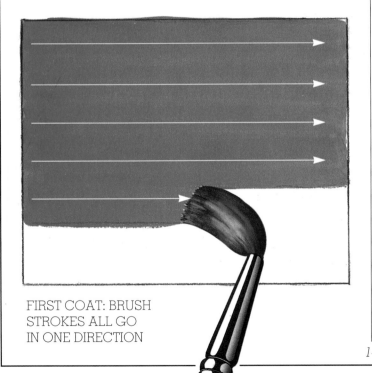

FIRST COAT: BRUSH
STROKES ALL GO
IN ONE DIRECTION

SECOND COAT: BRUSH
STROKES ALL GO IN THE
OPPOSITE DIRECTION

Light on dark

The logical order for applying tempera paint is: first, the dark colors, then the medium ones, and last the light ones.

However you paint, you must remember that to apply a color—either light or dark—over another one, you must wait until the first color is dry. If not, you must know exactly how they will blend together.

As you can see below on the left, tempera is opaque. For that reason, you must begin by applying a dark color first (A) and then superimposing a light color (B), completely covering the first coat. However, you must wait until the first coat has dried, before you apply the second coat.

You can also mix colors on the paper, as you can see in the two illustrations below. In this case, you must apply the second color before the first has dried and then mix them together with the brush.

A   B

COLOR APPLIED WITH
A LOT OF WATER

MIXED WITH
ANOTHER,
DRIER COLOR

How I paint...

A gradation with strips

Wet the color you've chosen for this exercise and paint a strip.

Add a little white to the color in the dish and paint another strip next to the first one.

Then add more white and paint another strip. Continue until you are working with pure white. But be careful—you must do all this as rapidly as possible, before the paint dries.

When all the strips are painted and while the tempera is still damp, moisten the brush slightly and pass it over the lines where the strips meet in order to get a uniform *gradation*.

GRADATION WITH WHITE
A. Paint a strip with the paint slightly wet. B. Paint successive strips, adding more white each time. C. Before the color dries, pass the almost dry brush over the edges of the strips to blend them together.

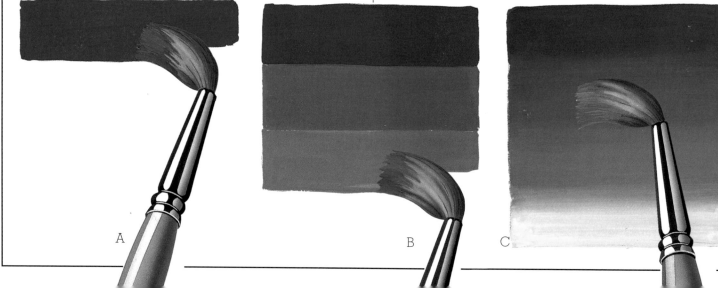

A

B

C

A gradation using water

Using light blue, wet the paint slightly so that the tempera is as thick as possible. Cover almost all the area to be gradated with the light blue, except for one edge. Now wet the dark blue and paint the edge you've left un-colored.

Join the light and dark blues by adding one to the other until you get a uniform gradation.

Correcting errors

Correcting mistakes in tempera is very risky. The color you want to change must be com-pletely dry. Generally, it is easier to repaint a large area, like a background, than to try to correct a small area.

When you do repaint an area, work the brushstrokes in the opposite direction from the original strokes.

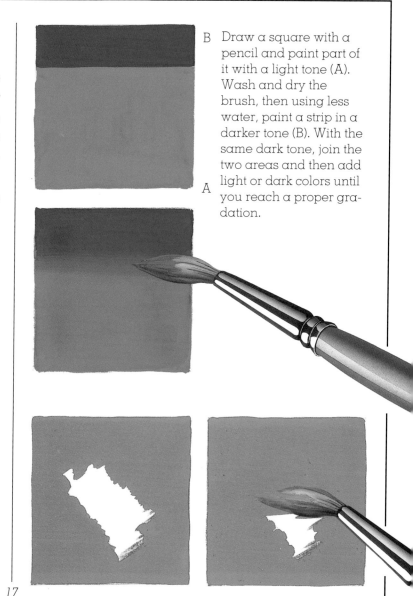

B Draw a square with a pencil and paint part of it with a light tone (A). Wash and dry the brush, then using less water, paint a strip in a darker tone (B). With the same dark tone, join the two areas and then add light or dark colors until you reach a proper gra-dation.

To correct mistakes, repaint the entire area with brushstrokes at right angles to the original strokes. But you must first wait until the color you want to cover is com-pletely dry.

Color...

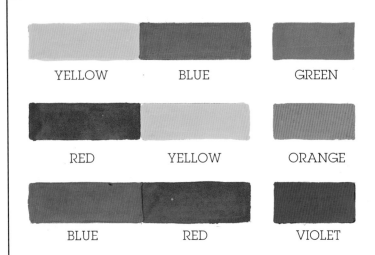

YELLOW · BLUE — GREEN

RED — YELLOW — ORANGE

BLUE — RED — VIOLET

The primary colors are: blue, yellow, and red. Mixing them, you get the secondary colors: green, orange, and violet.

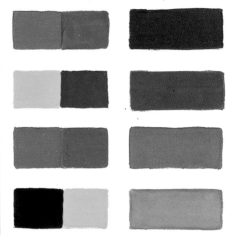

Practice mixing colors as much a possible, beginning with the examples on the left.

The basic colors

With your box of tempera, or your tubes or jars, you have a fairly wide assortment of colors.

But all these colors can be made by mixing just three of them. These are the three *primary colors*.

By mixing the primary colors—blue, yellow, and red—you get the *secondary colors*: green, orange, and violet.

By mixing the secondary colors, you get the *tertiary colors*: blue green, yellow green, yellow orange, red orange, red violet, and blue violet.

Practice mixing colors as much as possible. If necessary, use an entire box of paints experimenting. You can be sure it won't be a waste of time.

The color wheel

With the three primary colors, the three secondary colors, and the six tertiary colors we can make a chromatic *wheel.*

You can see that there are pairs

of colors connected by arrows. These are the *complementary colors.* The complementary colors provide the maximum color contrasts. For example, green is the complement of red, blue is the complement of orange, and so on.

The ranges of color

When combinations of colors are pleasing to look at, they are said to *harmonize.*

One way to harmonize colors is by using the ranges of *cool colors* and *warm colors.*

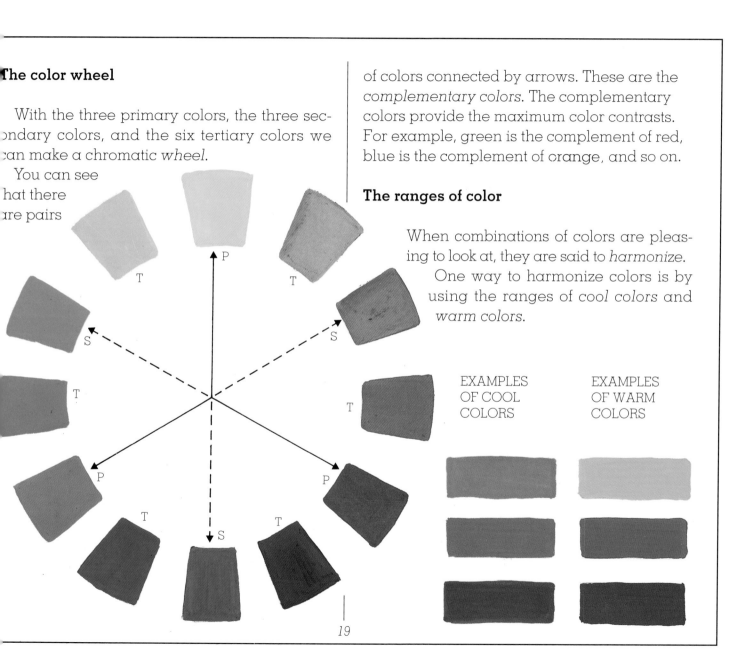

EXAMPLES OF COOL COLORS

EXAMPLES OF WARM COLORS

My first exercises...

Make a drawing of the basic shapes without pressing the pencil too hard on the paper.

You are going to practice using tempera without mixing colors yet. Apply the first layer of color.

Draw the main shape of the balloon, making a circle. Then draw the details

Paint all the stripes that are the same color and the basket. Be careful not to go outside the lines of the drawing.

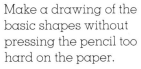

Use a fine brush to paint the stem and the leaves.

Don't apply any more color. When it is dry, paint darker tones, being careful not to mix the two colors.

Now paint the other colored strips and the other tone of the basket.

Once the color is dry, apply darker tones with a drier brush.

20

Now you will practice gradations. Draw the shape of the peach.

Wet the brush, pick up the paint, and apply a coat that is thinned with a lot of water.

This bird is not difficult to draw, but you must draw all the details.

First apply color to the areas of shadow.

Now use thicker paint to get darker tones.

Before the paint dries, make gradations with the lighter tone.

Mix each color with white and paint the light tones.

Now work on tonal contrast. Use a thicker paint on the shadows.

My first exercises...

This is a slightly more difficult exercise in which you will also be working on gradations. Draw the picture.

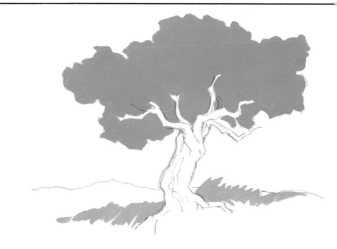

Apply a first coat of light green to the treetop. Add a little white and paint the grass.

Using light green and white, shade the upper part of the treetop until it blends with the color below. Paint the trunk.

Work quickly before the paint dries. Then, adding white, do the same thing to the trunk and the grass.

Draw the main shapes in the picture. This will give you a guide for applying the paint.

First color the cactuses, beginning with the lighter tones. Try to stay inside the pencil lines.

Paint the clay pot. When the color is dry, paint the darkest lines. Paint a few brushstrokes on the daisies and cactuses.

Work with white and dark green. With the fine brush, paint the daisies. Paint dark lines on the cactuses.

My first exercises...

Draw the *outline* of the tiger's head, the features of the face, and the stripes on the skin.

Apply a first coat, except for the eyes, ears, and a few areas around the *contour* of the head. Use loose strokes.

Lighten the color with white and mix this with the color you have already applied.

Paint the eyes, ears, and the stripes of the coat. Strengthen the areas of shadow.

24

With a soft pencil draw the outline of the bird and the branch. This will give you boundaries for the color.

With a slightly wet brush paint the feathers. With a fine brush do the same to the branch.

Now apply light colors to the head, breast, legs, and tail of the bird. Use different colors for the leaves.

Now blend the dark tones, mixing in a small amount of white. Mix the colors by going over them a few times with the brush.

My first exercises...

Outlining shapes is the most important part of drawing, but it is important to draw in all the details too.

Our next exercise is a *seascape* painted in flat colors with no gradations.

It is important that you draw this in as much detail as possible. Draw not only the outline of the boat, but also the details inside the boat, the horizon line, and the shadow of the boa on the sand.

When you paint the first coat of the sky, be careful to omit the area of the cloud.

In the dish mix light blue with a little yellow. Add some white and paint the base coat.
Wash the brush.
Take the same amount of yellow and violet with a little white and mix the colors in the dish. Paint the sand with horizontal brushstrokes. Before the paint dries, add another coat with vertical brushstrokes. This will give you a uniform tone.

My first exercises...

Paint the sea light blue with a little green.

Paint the lower part of the boat with violet, light blue, and a fair amount of white. Wash the brush and, using only white, paint the upper part of the boat, working on the area where the two colors meet.

With the same gray you've used on the boat, paint the lower part of the cloud.

For the sand, use violet, yellow, and blue.

With a fine brush, paint one of the lines of the boat red.

Add yellow to the gray of the boat to paint he inside.

Wet the brush and, using green and yellow, aint the line of the boat.

Paint the shadow at the front of the boat

with violet, red, and yellow. Add blue to the inside of the boat.

Use yellow for the mountain, and for a final effect, add a few touches of white to the bow of the boat.

My first exercises...

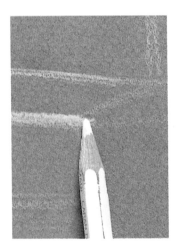

When you use colored paper, you must draw with a white pencil.

This exercise will be different—instead of white paper, you are going to use colored paper.

Painting on colored paper has its own characteristics. You can choose a color that harmonizes with the subject you'll be painting. That way part of the background can be the same color as the paper, which will give you a more pleasing effect.

First do the backgrounds.

Mix light blue and violet with a little white. Paint the entire area with vertical brushstrokes and then go over this coat again with horizontal brushstrokes.

Add green with some more white for the ground.

Paint the bushes light blue with a little green.

In some places let the color of the paper show.

My first exercises...

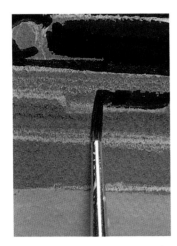

Use pure black for the strokes on the front part of the car.

Use black for the body.

Mix black with light blue for the shadows.

Use black for the outline of the windows and the tires.

Add enough white to make a light gray and paint the reflections in the windows.

Use gray also for the tires.

Add dark blue to the black to darken the bushes.

Use yellow with some white for the headlights. With a wet brush apply the yellow round the rims.

With a lot of white and a small amount of ellow, intensify the center of the headlights.

Paint one stripe on the car red and the other one light blue and white.

Paint the outline with blue adding more white. Use light blue, red, and black to darken the ground.

33

My first exercises...

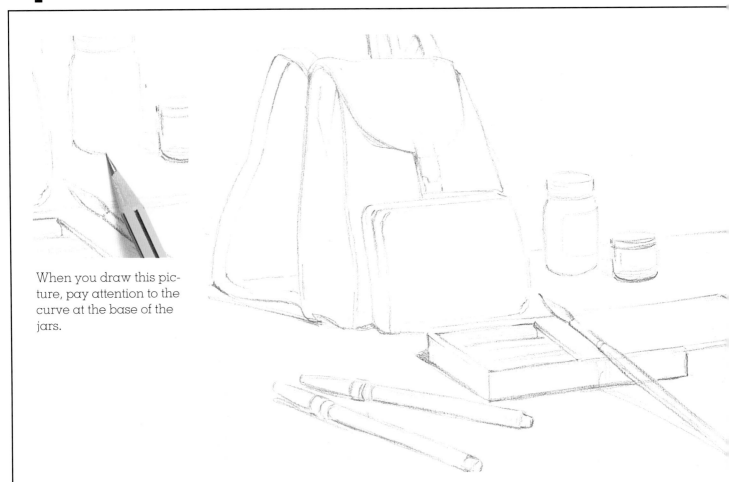

When you draw this picture, pay attention to the curve at the base of the jars.

The subject chosen for this exercise is a *still life* made up of very familiar objects.

However, now that you have to draw them, you will most probably discover that you don't know them as well as you thought. Don't let this discourage you!

In any case, it is better for you to use thi‹ drawing as a model before you try to draw th‹ actual objects.

Start with the background.

Mix light green with red, add white, and paint the back wall.

Wash the brush.

Then mix yellow and white and add a bit of red to paint the table.

You must paint quickly to spread the color, but be careful not to paint the objects.

My first exercises...

Use light green with a small amount of white for the side of the portfolio.

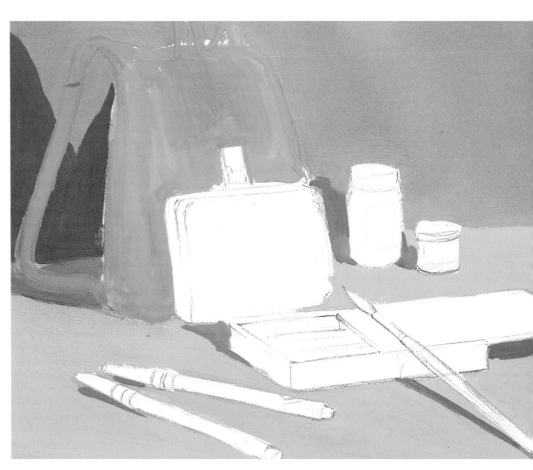

Darken the shadows by mixing dark green, violet and a little yellow.

Use violet with a small amount of green for the shadow on the table.

Apply a background to the portfolio, adding white to light green.

Apply all the brushstrokes in the same direction, without worrying about covering the pencil lines.

Use violet with a little white for the pocket of the portfolio.

Use green, red, and yellow for the pencil case.

Paint one marker red, using a lot of water.

Then mix white and light blue for the other marker.

Paint the brush handle black and the rest of the brush light blue and white. Paint one pot yellow and the other one dark blue.

My first exercises...

Paint the background wall with vertical brush-strokes to blend with the color underneath.

Mix dark green and dark blue and paint the shadow of the portfolio. Then tone it down by adding white.

Add a little red to light green to darken the strap.

Use violet with some dark blue for the shadow of the portfolio pocket.

Paint red, yellow, and light green on the background wall. Use ochre on one of the pots and paint a highlight on the other.

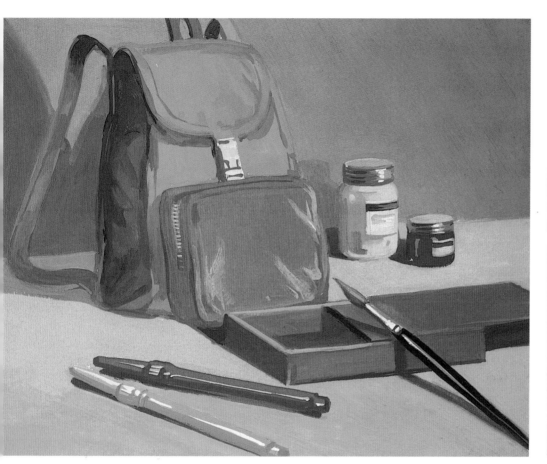

Make the gradation on the side of the portfolio by mixing dark blue with some dark green. To make the gradation, thin the paint by wetting the brush and drying it slightly with a paper towel.

With violet, yellow, and light green, you will get a dark brown for the sides and back of the pencil case.

My first exercises...

Draw the picture with a medium-soft (2B) graphite pencil. Your strokes will not mark the paper too deeply and will erase easily.

Our last exercise is a *landscape*. In it you will be able to practice everything you have learned.

First draw the picture. This time pay especial attention to the shapes.

As you can see, drawing the treetops, the trunks, and the houses take just a few lines.

Mix light blue with white and a little yellow. Then paint the background of the sky with horizontal brushstrokes, carefully outlining the treetops, the trunks, and the roofs of the houses. If you use your paint fairly thickly, it will be easy to get an even tone. Use violet and yellow for the fields in the foreground.

My first exercises...

Mix red, dark blue, and a little light green and paint the tree trunks with a fine brush.

Use yellow, light blue, and light green for the facades of the houses.

Apply a first coat to the treetops: Use light green with a very little yellow for one of them, and light green alone for the other.

Then paint the mountains with horizonta brushstrokes, mixing light blue, dark blue, and some purple.

Paint the cloud white mixed with blue, using more white on the upper part.

42

Over the background you have already painted, paint the field red. Then, before the paint dries, take a little yellow and mix both colors with rapid and decisive brushstrokes. Darken the treetops with dark green, espe-cially the lower parts. Then make a gradation of this color with light green.

43

My first exercises...

Where you want to blend the colors you must work over the areas again and again with your brush.

Continue making gradations of tones.

In the field, use light green, yellow, and a little violet.

Work on the darkest areas of the treetops. Mix light and dark green, and go over these areas until you have succeeded in blending the colors.

Use green and yellow for the lightest outlines of the tree trunks.

Add light green to the facade of one of the houses.

Continue working on the treetops: Use light green, dark green, and yellow in the lighter areas. Then add more yellow and blend it in,

making sure the paint is wet.

Mix light green and yellow for the trees in the background. Make dark lines in the trunks with a fine brush.

Glossary

chromatic circle. A circle made up of twelve colors: three primaries, three secondaries, and six tertiaries. Another name for chromatic circle is color wheel.

complementary colors. The secondary color obtained by mixing two primary colors, which is said to be complementary to the third primary color (for example, green, obtained by mixing blue and yellow, is complementary to red).

contour. The outline of a shape.

cool colors. Those that in the color wheel are located between green and violet, with both these colors included.

gouache. One of several names used for an opaque, water-based paint. (The others are tempera and poster color.)

gradation. The gradual shift from a darker tone to a lighter one or vice versa.

harmonize. Setting down colors so that none clashes with the others.

landscape. A drawing or painting of an inland scene. Subjects include mountains lakes, rivers, and snow scenes. In addition to natural elements, which dominate the picture, buildings, and people may be present.

opaque. A layer of paint that completely hides whatever color is underneath it.

outline. A quick sketch that with a few lines roughly sets down the basic elements of a subject.

palette. A thin board on which a painter mixes the color; also, the complete range of colors used by a particular artist.

poster paint. One of the several names used for an opaque, water-based paint. (The others are tempera and gouache.)

primary colors. Red, blue, and yellow; the colors that are blended to produce other colors, but that cannot themselves be obtained by any mixtures.

scale. A group of all the tone variations in a color.

secondary colors. Orange, purple, and green; the colors obtained by blending pairs of primary colors.

seascape. A drawing or painting of a scene at sea. Although natural elements dominate the picture, ships and people may also be present.

still life. A drawing or painting based on a collection of objects posed in a particular way by the artist.

tempera. One of several names used for an opaque, water-based paint. (The others are gouache and poster paints. Note that the term *tempera* is also used for an opaque paint in which the colored substances are mixed with egg yolk.)

tertiary colors. The colors obtained by blending a primary and secondary color (example, blue-green or red-orange).

tone. Intensities of a color, from the lightest to the darkest.

transparent. A layer of paint through which the color underneath can be seen.

warm colors. Those that in the color wheel are located between crimson and light yellow, with both these colors included.

watercolor. A transparent water-based paint.

Index